Snap books®

Miranda Cosgrove

by Heather E. Schwartz

Capstone press®

Mankato, Minnesota

Snap Books are published by Capstone Press,
151 Good Counsel Drive, P.O. Box 669, Mankato, Minnesota 56002.
www.capstonepress.com

Books published by Capstone Press are manufactured with paper
containing at least 10 percent post-consumer waste.

Library of Congress Cataloging-in-Publication Data
Schwartz, Heather E.
    Miranda Cosgrove / by Heather E. Schwartz.
    p. cm. — (Snap books. Star biographies)
    Summary: "Describes the life and career of Miranda Cosgrove" — Provided by publisher.
    Includes bibliographical references and index.
    ISBN 978-1-4296-3401-4 (library binding)
    1. Cosgrove, Miranda, 1993– — Juvenile literature. 2. Actors — United States — Biography — Juvenile literature.
I. Title. II. Series.
PN2287.C634S39 2010
791.4302'8092 — dc22   2009002747

Editor: Megan Peterson
Designer: Juliette Peters
Media Researcher: Marcie Spence

Photo Credits:
AP Images/Charles Sykes, 27; AP Images/Dawn Villella, 6; AP Images/Gus Ruelas, 23; AP Images/Lauren Greenfield/
VII, 18; AP Images/Tammie Arroyo, 7; Courtesy of Cindy Benedetti, Vice Principal at Maude Price Elementary School,
10; Getty Images Inc./Frederick M. Brown, 12; Getty Images Inc./George Napolitano/FilmMagic, 25; Getty Images Inc./
George Pimentel/WireImage, 9; Getty Images Inc./Matthew Peyton, 21; Getty Images Inc./Scott Burton/WireImage via
St. Jude Children's Research Hospital, 29; Getty Images Inc./SGranitz/WireImage, 15; Globe Photos, 11; Kevin Winter/
Getty Images for St. Jude, cover; Landov LLC/JOEL KOYAMA/MCT, 5; Newscom/Handout/MCT, 17

Essential content words are **bold** and are defined at the bottom of the page where they first appear.

Table of Contents

CHAPTER 1

Not-So-Typical Teen

In June 2008, Miranda Cosgrove visited the Mall of America in Bloomington, Minnesota. Wearing purple pants with a black short-sleeved shirt and vest, she went to Nordstrom. Miranda tried on summer hats and Ed Hardy sneakers in size seven. She sampled lipsticks, found a color she liked, and made a purchase. It didn't bother her when some shoppers asked to take a photo with her. After all, Miranda wasn't really at the mall to shop.

Surrounded by security guards, Miranda left the store and headed toward a symphony of sounds. What was the source of all that noise? More than 600 people were screaming with excitement. They had gathered to see the star of Nickelodeon's hit show *iCarly*. Now there was no way Miranda could pretend she was just a regular teen out shopping.

Miranda tried on lipstick before a CD signing at the Mall of America.

"As long as I can remember, I've always wanted to sing and act, so for me to be able to do what I'm doing is so cool. It's definitely a dream come true."
— Miranda talks about her success, from an interview with *People* magazine.

Miranda smiled and waved at her fans, who held signs decorated with her photo. They snapped her picture with digital cameras and cell phones. Miranda walked onto a stage and sat behind a long table. Then she started autographing copies of her debut album, *iCarly: Music From and Inspired by the Hit TV Show*. Miranda chatted easily with her fans. She complimented their outfits and even gave out hugs.

For another girl, the whole event might have been stressful. For Miranda, it was just one day in a life she loves.

Miranda, shown here at the March 2008 opening of Nickelodeon Universe at the Mall of America, enjoys meeting her fans.

Free-Thinking Fashionista

As an actress and singer, Miranda's job includes making public appearances. At the 2008 Teen Choice Awards, she got on stage to present an award. While her fellow presenters wore brightly colored strapless numbers, Miranda went a different route.

Miranda chose a conservative jumper dress with a black top, gray miniskirt, and suspenders. She painted her nails black to match. A wide, red cuff bracelet added a dash of color on her wrist. Miranda stepped out in black heels with her long hair flowing free. She looked equal parts cute, classy, and sassy.

Miranda was excited to be a presenter at the 2008 Teen Choice Awards.

Born under a Lucky Star

On May 14, 1993, Miranda Taylor Cosgrove was born in Downey, California. Downey is near Los Angeles, where the entertainment industry thrives. Miranda's dad, Tom, owns a dry cleaning business. Her mom, Chris, is a stay-at-home mom. Miranda is an only child.

Luck struck when Miranda was just 3 years old. Her parents took her to a local restaurant called Taste of L.A. They didn't know it, but a talent **agent** happened to be dining there. Just for fun, Miranda started singing and dancing around the tables. The agent was impressed. She asked Miranda's parents if she could sign their daughter to a contract.

Miranda's parents never considered letting their only child work in entertainment. Chris wasn't sure it was a good idea. But she could see how much her daughter enjoyed performing, even at a young age. Miranda's parents talked it over and signed her with an agent. At age 3, Miranda began her career.

agent — someone who helps actors find work

Miranda, shown here at age 10, enjoyed performing from a young age.

Miranda's first **audition** was for a Mello Yellow commercial. She won the role. Even as a tot, Miranda had talent plus a polite attitude. She proved it by winning early roles in commercials for McDonald's and Burger King. She also worked as a child model.

Schooltime

Miranda's budding career didn't change her life much. Until fifth grade, she attended Maude Price Elementary School in Downey, California. There she made friends who would stick by her even after she became a star. For fun she acted in school plays and took singing lessons. She often stayed up late doing homework and always got good grades. She was also into movies, music, horseback riding, and fencing.

Miranda attended Maude Price Elementary School in Downey, California.

audition — a tryout performance for an actor

Miranda (second from right) played an uptight band manager in *School of Rock*.

The Making of a Movie Star

After a few years of modeling and acting in commercials, Miranda knew she really enjoyed performing. She took acting lessons and sought out more challenging roles. Miranda and her parents read scripts sent by her agent. Together they chose roles that were appropriate and tasteful.

When she was 9, Miranda filmed a **pilot** for a new Nickelodeon show called *Drake & Josh*. She also competed against thousands of other kids for a role in the movie *School of Rock*. To prepare for her movie audition, Miranda memorized her lines and practiced them with her parents. Miranda auditioned three times. Then producers asked her to audition in front of the camera. Two weeks later, Miranda won the role of Summer Hathaway in *School of Rock*.

pilot — a sample episode of a planned TV show

In *School of Rock*, Jack Black played a substitute teacher who turned his fifth grade class into a rock band. The lead roles for kids included a bass player, a guitarist, a drummer, and a keyboard player. Miranda's character, Summer, was the one kid who wasn't musical. Summer sang a few lines of the song "Memories" to convince her teacher she should be in the band. Summer's singing was awful. The teacher made her the band manager instead. Miranda took a 45-minute singing lesson to learn how to sing badly.

Miranda (second row, third from right) attended the first Hollywood showing of *School of Rock*.

On the Set

Miranda was the youngest of the kids with lead roles in the movie. But she was the only actor among them with professional experience. Filming took place in New York City. While on set, the kids worked with an on-set teacher for a few hours each day. Miranda liked working with funnyman Jack Black. She and her young costars were later nominated at the Young Artists Awards for Best Young **Ensemble** in a Feature Film.

After filming the movie, Miranda had a new interest in classic rock. She listened to her mom's old albums. She even discovered a band she really liked, The Rolling Stones.

Miranda's First Movie Date

When Miranda was in fifth grade, she went to see a Harry Potter movie with a major crush. In the middle of the movie, things turned romantic. Miranda's crush was about to plant a kiss on her cheek.

Suddenly, her friend whacked the back of the boy's head! The friend was just being protective, but the moment passed. Miranda didn't get a kiss or a boyfriend out of the deal. But she did stay friends with her former crush. Years later, she laughed telling a reporter that the boy still teased her about their missed kiss.

ensemble — a group of musicians or actors who perform together

Now Starring Miranda

Miranda was filming *School of Rock* when she found out *Drake & Josh* was set to become a weekly show. The show is about stepbrothers Drake and Josh. Drake, played by Drake Bell, is a fun-loving guitar player. Josh, played by Josh Peck, is a serious type who follows the rules. They're complete opposites but have to share their family and even their room.

For three years, Miranda played the role of Megan Parker, Drake's **mischievous** little sister. Miranda became good friends with costars Drake and Josh. She considers them family. During breaks between scenes, they liked to play tricks on each other. Drake once filled Miranda's bathroom with shaving cream! To even the score, Miranda filled his shoes with shaving cream.

mischievous — able or tending to cause trouble in a playful way

Miranda attended the 18th annual Kids' Choice Awards in Los Angeles with costars Drake Bell and Josh Peck (left to right).

15

Busy Star

Miranda had steady work on *Drake & Josh*. In 2005, she also filmed the movie *Yours, Mine & Ours* starring Dennis Quaid and Rene Russo. Miranda was cast as Joni North and had to play saxophone in the movie. Miranda took saxophone lessons to prepare for the role. The film's paint fight was Miranda's favorite scene to shoot. The cast threw colored cake batter and pudding instead of real paint. Miranda says they couldn't stop eating the fake paint!

That same year, Miranda voiced the character of Munch in the animated film *Here Comes Peter Cottontail: The Movie*. Molly Shannon and Kenan Thompson also voiced characters in the movie.

"I love going to the mall and when kids come up and say the episodes they like the most and which ones made them laugh. It's really cool."
— Miranda talks about her *iCarly* fans, from an interview with *Scholastic News Online*.

A Show of Her Own

Drake & Josh ended in 2007. Miranda wasn't sure what would come next. Her agent sent her scripts to read. She auditioned for roles in movies and on TV. Then came a happy surprise. Nickelodeon decided to develop a show specifically for Miranda.

Miranda was 14 when she started playing Carly Shay, the lead role on *iCarly*. On the show, Carly creates a webcast that becomes an instant hit with viewers. *iCarly* also became an instant hit when it debuted in September 2007. Miranda liked playing a well-rounded character who has boy problems and fights with friends. Miranda also got to meet cool guest stars, like the band Good Charlotte and *American Idol* star David Archuleta. *iGo to Japan*, an *iCarly* TV movie, debuted in November 2008.

Nathan Kress (far left) and Jennette McCurdy (far right) play Freddie and Sam on *iCarly*.

Professional hairstylists and makeup artists make sure Miranda looks her best when filming *iCarly*.

Changes

Starring in her own TV show changed Miranda's life. She still hung out with the friends she'd made in elementary school. But she also had schoolwork to complete. After fifth grade, Miranda was homeschooled and then tried online school. While working on *iCarly*, Miranda and the cast rehearsed for three days each week. On rehearsal days, Miranda had four hours of on-set tutoring. Miranda had only one hour of tutoring during the two days of filming.

If her new school schedule didn't remind Miranda that her life was unusual, there were other signs. When she went to the mall or the movies, fans spotted her. They came over to talk, sometimes in crowds.

In interviews, the **media** asked how she was handling her fame. Would she go wild now that she was a teen star? Miranda disagreed. She enjoyed hanging out with friends and going to movies. And Miranda's mom was always on the set. Her dad stopped by as often as he could.

Blooper Moment

Being in front of an audience is normal for Miranda. But that doesn't mean she always performs perfectly. While filming a scene for her TV show *iCarly*, Miranda had to wear a robe and fuzzy slippers. Then she had to race up to two other actors. About 50 other actors were also on the set.

When Miranda ran over, she slipped and fell. Everyone turned to stare. In her words, it was "the most embarrassing thing ever."

media — TV, radio, newspapers, and other communication forms that send out messages to large groups of people

A Growing Career

Miranda was 15 when she started her second season of the hit show *iCarly*. Early on the producers of *iCarly* asked Miranda to sing the show's theme song. Miranda recorded "Leave It All To Me." This was her first time in a recording studio. She was eager to do it again.

Miranda soon got that chance. The producers decided to make an album of songs from and inspired by the show. The album featured well-known artists including Avril Lavigne, Natasha Bedingfield, Sean Kingston, and The Naked Brothers Band. Miranda sang the theme song and recorded three new tunes.

Miranda experienced another first when she filmed her first music video. "Stay My Baby" **premiered** on Nickelodeon during an episode of *SpongeBob SquarePants* in August 2008. Some of Miranda's friends joined her in the "About You Now" video. Miranda's early music lessons and years of practice were starting to pay off.

premiere — the first public performance of a film, play, or work of music or dance

Miranda toured the United States to promote the *iCarly* album.

The *iCarly* album gave Miranda a chance to prove she really was acting when she sang poorly in *School of Rock*. In the summer of 2008, *iCarly* debuted at number one on the Billboard Top Kid Audio albums chart. The album also debuted at number one on the SoundScan Top Children's Current album sales chart.

Miranda Goes Solo

Even before the *iCarly* album came out, Miranda started work on a new project — her first solo album. Miranda didn't have the opportunity to write songs for the *iCarly* album. This time she wanted to use her songwriting skills. At first Miranda worried about saying the wrong thing in a song. She soon realized being afraid could hold her back. Miranda wrote songs about love and hanging out with friends. She was excited to show fans a different, more mature Miranda. *About You Now,* a five-song digital album, was released on iTunes in February 2009.

Eye Carly

iCarly gives fans a chance to show off their talents and be part of the show. Fans can upload their own videos to the *iCarly* Web site. Miranda and the show's producers watch the videos and choose their favorites to appear in episodes of the show.

Like her fans, Miranda has her own hidden talent. She can shake her eyes! "I think I have extra eye muscles," she's said. Since then, she's performed her trick on *The Today Show* for a national audience.

Drake & Josh Reunion

In 2008 Miranda **reprised** her role as Megan Parker in the TV movie *Merry Christmas, Drake & Josh*. The movie got its own red-carpet premiere in Los Angeles. Miranda posed with Santa Claus, talked with reporters, and greeted fans. *Merry Christmas, Drake & Josh* debuted on December 5, 2008. With 8.1 million viewers, it became Nickelodeon's highest-rated live-action movie.

Miranda looked stylish in a black dress with hot-pink stripes at the premiere of *Merry Christmas, Drake & Josh.*

reprise — to repeat the performance

CHAPTER 5

Following Her Own Path

As Miranda Cosgrove became a household name, she was often compared to Miley Ray Cyrus. The comparison didn't bother her a bit. In fact, Miranda took the comparison as a compliment. Miranda's role models include Gwen Stefani, Anne Hathaway, and Rachel McAdams. McAdams starred in one of Miranda's favorite movies *Mean Girls*. But Miranda doesn't try to model her career after anyone else's. She enjoys doing her own thing.

"I don't think acting is a big deal. To be honest, I'm just an ordinary teen. I do the regular stuff with my buddies like watching movies, having sleepovers, and shopping."
— Miranda, from an interview with *The Star Online*.

Miranda gets invited to appear on other TV shows, like MTV's *Total Request Live*.

Life of a Teen Star

Miranda sets herself apart from many young stars by staying grounded and remaining true to herself. Fame granted Miranda an extraordinary life. But it doesn't make her act like a diva. Miranda talks openly about her wholesome lifestyle. She likes to play tennis, ride her bike, and go to the movies. Miranda admits to spending a lot of time watching TV. Her favorite shows are *Grey's Anatomy*, *America's Next Top Model*, and *American Idol*. And she loves animals. Miranda's pets include adopted stray kittens and her toy poodle, Pearl.

Life as a celeb comes with plenty of perks. Miranda loves to shop, especially for vintage clothes. She bought the new iPhone and texts her pals whenever she has a free moment. Miranda also attends glamorous red-carpet events and takes trips around the world. She even got to meet her celebrity crush, Shia LeBeouf, at the 2008 Teen Choice Awards.

For the most part, Miranda enjoys life in the spotlight. But her parents don't treat her differently just because she is a famous actress. Miranda still has to clean her room and finish her homework on time. She even gets grounded if she breaks the rules. When out with friends, Miranda must be home by 11:00 at night.

Miranda performed "About You Now" during the 2008 Macy's Thanksgiving Day Parade in New York City.

Being famous does have its drawbacks. Miranda doesn't like online discussions where her name is mentioned. While plenty of fans love Miranda, some people aren't so supportive. They think it's okay to write mean messages about Miranda simply because she's famous. Her friends often stick up for her in those chats. That makes Miranda feel better.

Cool, Calm, and Collected

Miranda is a young actress. But that doesn't mean she isn't a professional. Miranda is always on time for work, photo shoots, and interviews. She doesn't surround herself with an army of hairstylists and makeup artists. And she doesn't cruise around town in a limo. Instead Miranda and her parents travel to events in the family car.

Miranda's polite and professional attitude earned her the *iCarly* gig. Dan Schneider, the show's producer, also created *Drake & Josh*. Schneider knew Miranda had what it took to headline her own show. He says that Miranda never complains and is one of the classiest actresses around.

Helping Others

Being a celebrity isn't all acting, singing, and wearing cute clothes to awards shows. Miranda also spends time giving back to the fans who have made her so popular. In 2008, she visited St. Jude Children's Research Hospital in Memphis, Tennessee. Miranda was joined by the Jonas Brothers and actor Angus T. Jones.

Miranda spent the day signing autographs, posing for pictures, chatting with patients, and coloring art projects with them. She did it all with a smile that showed she was happy to be there.

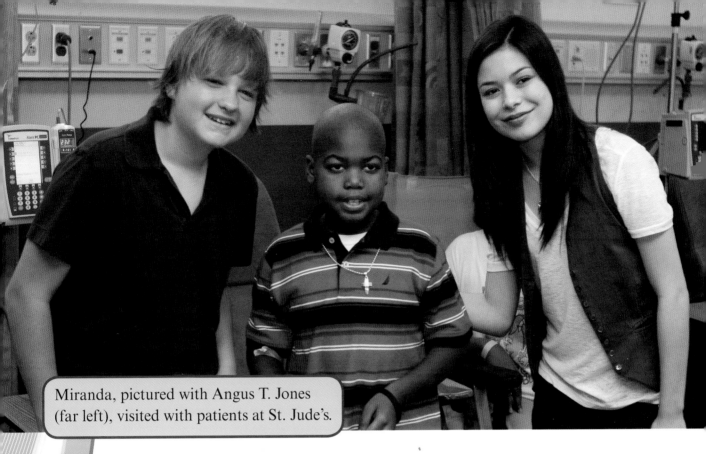

Miranda, pictured with Angus T. Jones (far left), visited with patients at St. Jude's.

Into the Future

Miranda's future plans include more acting and singing. Her next movie, the animated feature *Despicable Me*, hits theaters in 2010. Celebs Steve Carell, Jason Segal, and Julie Andrews also voiced characters in the movie. Miranda hopes to star in a comedy and an independent film. And she plans to headline her own concert tour.

College is also in Miranda's future plans. She's interested in the University of Southern California and New York University. Either way, Miranda would like to study marine biology.

Whatever she decides to do, Miranda is sure to approach new challenges with her signature sunny attitude. Growing up as a celebrity has taught Miranda how to show the world her very best.

Glossary

agent (AY-juhnt) — someone who helps actors find work

audition (aw-DISH-uhn) — a tryout performance for an actor

ensemble (on-SOM-buhl) — a group of musicians or actors who perform together

media (MEE-dee-uh) — TV, radio, newspapers, and other communication forms that send out messages to large groups of people

mischievous (MISS-chuh-vuhss) — able or tending to cause trouble in a playful way

pilot (PYE-luht) — a sample episode of a planned TV show

premiere (pruh-MIHR) — the first public performance of a film, play, or work of music or dance

reprise (ree-PRIZE) — to repeat the performance

vintage (VIN-tij) — from the past

wholesome (HOLE-suhm) — suggesting good health, a sound mind, or good or moral behavior

Read More

Franks, Katie. *Miranda Cosgrove.* Kid Stars! New York: PowerKids Press, 2009.

Jones, Jen. *Being Famous.* 10 Things You Need to Know About. Mankato, Minn.: Capstone Press, 2008.

Leavitt, Amie Jane. *Miranda Cosgrove.* A Robbie Reader. Hockessin, Del.: Mitchell Lane, 2009.

Ryals, Lexi. *Miranda Mania: An Unauthorized Biography.* New York: Price Stern Sloan, 2008.

Internet Sites

FactHound offers a safe, fun way to find Internet sites related to this book. All of the sites on FactHound have been researched by our staff.

Here's all you do:

Visit *www.facthound.com*

FactHound will fetch the best sites for you!

Index